ON OCCASION

Books by Joel Oppenheimer

POEMS

    The Dutiful Son
    The Love Bit
    In Time

PLAY

    The Great American Desert

NON-FICTION

    The Wrong Season

6.95

ON OCCASION.

some births,
deaths,
weddings,
birthdays,
holidays,
and other events

poems by
JOEL OPPENHEIMER

THE BOBBS-MERRILL COMPANY, INC.
Indianapolis – New York

PS
3529
. P6905

Thanks are due to the Creative Artists Public Service Program
for financial assistance which helped make this book possible.

Published by the Bobbs-Merrill Company, Inc.
Indianapolis   New York

ISBN 0–672–51719–1 Hardcover
ISBN 0–672–51720–5 Paperback
Library of Congress catalog card number 73–1721
Designed by Nancy Dale Muldoon
Manufactured in the United States of America

First printing

this book is for

        FRANZ KLINE
        and
        CHARLES OLSON
            "too much is not enough"

CONTENTS

birthdays

holidays

OTHER EVENTS

life

LIBERTY

art

politics

THE PURSUIT OF HAPPINESS

fun

games

A PREFATORY NOTE

the earliest of these poems was written in 1950, remembering a sad occasion of my childhood; the latest was written the other day, commenting on a bad choice of mine for breakfast provender.

which is what occasional poetry is about: the celebration and/or mourning of the occasions of one's life.

goethe says somewhere that occasional poetry is the highest form of art; when it succeeds i incline to agree with him— by success i mean when the poem moves past the personal impetus for writing it, but preserves the solid air of that impetus; in other words, that the poem, hopefully, may be meaningful far beyond the immediate situation.

occasional poems also indicate, for me, a "usefulness" for poetry as a function of life and a benefit to society that belies popular rumor.

OCCASIONS

Births

FOR DAVID

eyes wide, we
have dumped it
in your lap. you
do not know that
yet. hands open
and closed, the
panorama stretches
before you. you
do not know that
yet. lips ready,
you will take all
we have to give you.
and will survive.
and will pay us
back in our own
coin. even love,
if we come to deserve it.

FOR A CHRISTENING

t. j. quinn, 11 january 1969

what we have here is
a small round cap, a
yommikah, or, in my
childhood, a koppalah.

3

it is blue, and hidden
on the surface is
dark old gold braid.
it started moving toward
you as a joke and
then i reconsidered.
after all, a mad mick
father, another long
island mockey mom,
friends like pete
and me, you'll need
all the help you can
find, in this harsh world.

so take it, keep it
somewhere handy, remember
those heritages that
can help you, the church
and the shul—that
this small hat, for
instance, reminds us
the jews alone will not
remove their hat, even
for g-d, even when they
are talking to h-m.

grow your own strengths,
learn to move to the
left well, get the
good hands, do all
those things we need, even,
if it comes to that,
become a doctor, but
remember always the two
blessings you have been
blessed with, the holy
trinity, and the omnipotent
one, remember that lammad-vov,

the hidden saint no one
suspects, who crept in
and blessed you also.

grow well, in peace,
and love.

A BIRTH

for kristin, may 1969

born, a girl, in this
wild age. oh well, did
you expect better from
the world? we are made
the way we are and grow
likewise, attracting whatever
forces stew around us.
personally speaking, i
have never much trusted
your sex—except in
the areas necessary, so
i can give you love salted
with the proper respect
and say i am glad you
are here. women are more
useful than we guessed when
young, and we have learned
to welcome you. be
blessed and grow happy,
observe whatever of this
world we leave to you,
and make it flower.

A POEM FOR CHILDREN

the headline in the
poet's voice and intelligencer says
tom and paul have boys. we all
dance around the maypole, it
being that month and appropriate.
i have seen only little tom,
carlos t. awaits as he did for
nine months. i am assured
joanie looked beautiful two days
before term, a term they use. the
children will grow up my friends.

in itself a curious act, growing
up has been defined not once but
several times. not once did they
mention helicopters. not once did
they mention god being on the wrong
side, or the possibility of total
grace for a child who can't say the
word "park," no less "people's park."
they will grow up playing somehow and
finding their toys, even if the toys
are guns and the heads of their enemies:

for love, i would
split open, etc.

and if the toys destroy, who
asked for it? who taught it? my own
son smiled today to see me ask him
not to throw the ball—over went
the jug of water on the floor. i
yelled. he cried. i think that
he will live.
what we are saying is
these children, born, are not going

to eat shit; i have a better hope for
it than ever—tom mcgrath is over
fifty! paul blackburn is over forty! joel
oppenheimer is over thirty! they are
breeding children! those children
will have children to learn from!
they will be immune from teargas!
they will come happily! even when
young! they will be able to like
tits without being hung up on them!
they will recognize cops in one-fifth
of a bartender's time! they will
even know how to play in parks! they
will even know how to shoot down
helicopters over the parks!

well, it's a dream, little tom,
carlos t., and nathaniel. i can't even
make you a school. i am trying.
someday maybe this world will be ready
for you, o knowledgeable of the earth.
someday maybe the world will say to
you where were you? we were waiting!
here is a sliding pond, slide down it;
here are swings, go swing on them.
i do not think so, but i will try
to give you some strength to do it,
all the while watching fervently the
skies, the helicopters, and the cops.

Deaths

POEM

listen:
how many people listen when the hound howls?
when my uncle died and the people all were sad
they sat around his coffin and the hound sat
on top. for seven days
they sat darkened in the room with the hound howling
on top. clothes were ripped without pretense;
ties they'd never wear. they
sat around the coffin on hard benches and
they moaned and whispered and said they heard him
howl.
they let me walk in and see my uncle dead.
seeing them i felt i had to cry, to
say i saw the hound, but when i walked in
to see my uncle dead i heard a bark and i stopped
crying and i laughed instead because
my uncle once had shown me in december that
the way to warm your hands was to
blow through them clasped. we were happy then.

FOR WILLIAM CARLOS WILLIAMS

i am angry because
there are still
birthdays
          and yet they
tell me you
are bad off . that

you are dying
                    that
the last time you
went off they
thought you
were gone
                    (at the
same time they
say you are
furiously
jealous—
                    that someone
else can still
use a
right hand!

they tell me you
are an old man

they say when
you write new
verse they will not
take the
last one until
you write
the next
                    they are
afraid you
will decide it
is all you
have to say.

it is
difficult to
talk about

:   how much land
you moved
into

9

        it is an old
story
no one is much
interested
                especially
in the face of it
that you are
still at
it.

the inheritance
will not be written
down and cannot be
contested

which is why there
is a need to
say something to
you . said straight
out without the
dignity of
image even—
                since if
you are dying then
you do not need
images now . rather
we should save
things to put
next to you which
you loved and
needed

that it should be
a good trip
                that you should
still be able to
move as it
was

(old man i
am living on
that land, developing
it, i.e., raising
houses and
cutting the timber

—like a dutiful
son the father
hates

—and it
makes me ashamed
sitting here
                    no
matter how
busily

FOR MATTHEW, DEAD

8 august 1967

at four, it seems to me, he
fell off the stump by the
mess hall, bruising the
hell out of his forehead
and nose, and a good deal
of screaming went on.

how shall we scream now,
when at twenty, he slipped
on a wet, moss-covered
ledge of north percy peak
and fell one hundred yards to

11

his death. at least this
made that decision for him:
he will neither serve in
lyndon's army, nor go to
jail, nor go to canada.
he was trying to scale the
peak by the west trail.

one half hour ago my own
son at eight months fell,
tripping in his walker over
a raised lip of door.
it will not appear on the
book page of the *times*,
and we laughed instead of
screaming, to soothe him
down. this one has almost
eighteen years to make
his choice, and every day
a peril. good christ,
there are easier ways to
have decisions made. twenty
is no good time to die.

FOR MY WIFE'S GRANDFATHER, DEAD

12 november 1967

jews! bury him quietly.
we do that.
              we do not
carry on like the
goyim.
          he was an old
man. he lived a long

life. he lived a
hard life. he bred
a family. he is
dead now. we bury him
quickly, and in silence,
it is all he would ask.

pomp for him would be
lying, hillel said an
hour of good works on
earth is worth all the
eternity that might be.

his good works exist,
the hour and more.
bury him quietly.

FOR A MAN

leon seidel, 19 may 1968

we argued about who
got more space, and
when i scored the
new yorker he was
properly impressed
and bounced back with
wins. now he has
three-quarters of a
column in the *times*.

we put him down as
we do any man, and
he could take it;

13

we laughed at the
financier, and we
all bought yellowknife.
and if it was a
fight with the phone
company or con-ed
his eyes lit up
and he straightened
it out.
              we sat there
last night, the door
locked, and everybody
did it their own way:
schlenk drunk, me
unable to, the kob
screaming, mike
dazed—we all did
it our own way, because
after all it is
grief and grief must
be handled. even
cynically, and i
understand that too.

then someone said, oh
god, a thousand
people to be called
with that call—
and that is the
measure of him, that
a thousand people
cared. good-bye, friend.

TWO DEATHS

david stern
rfk
6 june 1968

the private grief and the public grief.
this old man is dead.
he was found in his private hell
by his children, unable to move or
call for help. and the other also
lay unconscious, and he died also.
all the time i bounce between the
private grief and the public grief.
it does not help much, but nothing
does that, these days. at least,
he had lived a long time, adamantly
refusing any help, anything that
would make him less of his own man,
and he was loved for that. the
apartment was filled with the pictures
that were his only intimates for
thirty years—his own grandchildren
had never seen the inside of this
room. he visited, he loved, he gave
of himself, but this much he held
for himself—pictures, a favorite
chair, the dining room table his
daughter was raised at. i mean
no complaint, but it does not help
that the death of the other was
a national tragedy, a national disgrace.

ANOTHER OLD MAN GONE

this one we'll miss, as he
gawks his way along, men-
acing, and i wasn't allowed
to see him.
                    the police ser-
geant arresting him,
he said: i can bring him
back to life. better a
conviction than a live man,
said the thirties—and yet
i always wanted to hear what
the old man would say about
the heart transplants. i
like to think it would be:
fellas, i was only acting.

i wish they hadn't scared
the shit out of me when i
was young. still, given
the strange age, people breaking
their ass, what else should
we have expected.

glomp glomp glomp he moves
in our dreams; he sits his
mother carefully before the
horrible machine, he says
hold still mother it won't
hurt you a bit. it didn't.
the fuzz were wrong! the
villagers were wrong! the
aristocrats were wrong!
boris karloff never hurt
nobody! boris karloff even

died carrying a cross out to
assuage the arabs!
                          he was
an old man, eighty-one,
and he had his own heart.

LEO OPPENHEIMER

8 august 1969

i went to see my father dying.
there is a man on the moon.
he liked to argue a lot, about politics.
when the man walked out of the capsule
there was a guy on a baseball team
trying to get a hit. he cared
about baseball. that was because
he was all-american, a pure strain.
he voted for debs in one election
and nixon in another. he was a
lower-middle-class business man
and when he got rich we got a new house
and limoges china and good sterling
silver whose name i forget and a
mink coat for my mother. we were
jews. he sucked his life out on cigarettes
and commuting and the pain in the
ass of raising a family when families
shouldn't have been raised, and he
read books. sat there while the family
raged and screamed in its own silent
way and read books. and taught his
sons to read books. and sat there silent

except when he argued, screamed, telling
cousin mac his son was not a communist, he
was an anarchist. you could live with that.
and then they said don't talk, don't
walk. what is a man supposed to do,
stop it all?
           he did his duty to
god and man as he saw fit and i
have to be embarrassed as i think to
pay my homage. he was my father.

THE POLISH CAVALRY

for chas. olson, 1 january 1970

they stood there, in the mud,
one hundred thousand of them,
waiting for the panzers, and
they got it. there are certain
monoliths taught us something.
the estaurine ranges to thirty
feet, god knows how long he will
survive. what i am trying to say is
that you brought two generations
to life, and you'll have to
live with that. you always did move
like a grampus and you still do.
the polish cavalry at least had lances.
what you've got only your sons and
your grandsons know. the map of
the battle of the cowpens shows
what can be done with only a few
men, will you believe that now,
in your time of need? i'm sorry

i have to speak in different images,
but you told me a long time ago
to speak in my own, and i believed
that. you still are the man who
held a full pall mall like i
hold the stub of a gauloise, and though you
think you are prometheus, his liver
pecked at, for me you are odin.
let them take out an eye and give you
a gray cloak. you have saved us.

OBITUARY

paul de kruif you
are dead i read in
the *times* tuesday
march second, and
i am brought
back nine years
old reading my
brother's library the
microbe hunters how
i wanted to believe
it was all there,
koch over his
cultures, ehrlich
peering at
slides they were
going to make us
all healthy no more
diseases something went
wrong in our uni
verse but i wanted
then to believe and
did and dreamed of
all that could be

19

conquered a little
boy nine years old how
can i tell anyone what
you meant more than
albert payson ter
hune who after all just
talked of pets and
green fields and
loyalty, you talked of
killers and men who
saved us slaving in
laboratories oh
wernher von braun and
whoever invented
nerve gas when will
i read your obituaries
in the *new york times*
as the kids gather for
another workshop trying
to write a poem that
will save us from
diseases, despite
the obvious pun i
have my own koch
institute paul de
kruif and we are
hoping to find some
magic bullet, we
are hoping the answer is
as simple as finding
the problem with
the blood and how
to cure it, to cure
the ills of man.

Weddings

HOKKU 237b

for tony and ruth, 10 january 1960

violets. winter
sun thru blinds.
                 light strikes hard, soft,
warms the violets.

A PRAYER

for a wedding, 29 november 1963

because everyone knows exactly what's good for another
because very few see
because a man and a woman may just possibly look at each
          other
because in the insanity of human relationships there still
          may come a time we say: yes, yes
because a man or a woman can do anything he or she
          pleases
because you can reach any point in your life saying: now, i
          want this
because eventually it occurs we want each other, we want
          to know each other, even stupidly, even uglily
because there is at best a simple need in two people to try
          and reach some simple ground

21

because that simple ground is not so simple
because we are human beings gathered together whether
        we like it or not
because we are human beings reaching out to touch
because sometimes we grow
            we ask a blessing on this marriage
            we ask that some simplicity be allowed
            we ask their happiness
            we ask that this couple be known for what it is,
                and that the light shine upon it
            we ask a blessing for their marriage

A RULE

for bruce and roxanne on their wedding,
27 march 1965

we become what we are is
how i said it. what, she
said? is that what you mean?
yes. we become what we are,
and have to spend hard times
learning it. the me that
kicked his way alive starts
just now to breathe, and the
thirty-five years long gone
pursuing some other self will
just be chalked up—no use,
the man said, crying over
spilt years, or time under
the bridge. now I have uncovered
that naked babe howling his
self alive, and i am through
with the other shapes. the
masks are usable, but i
know i am using them.

22

A SONG FOR TWO VOICES

for ted and joan wilentz
on their wedding, 25 june 1965

        voices in the silence, quiet
        in the voice,
                    since our first
        beginning, cause enough for joy

we meet seldom enough in
quiet that it becomes
needed: peace, peace
in our time, with some
space for reflection
                    and
it's good, also, to rest
easy, after a long run, with
too much talking. it's
good to build up again some
reason for speaking, some
reason for reaching out a
simple hand—the simple
gesture it takes to make
contact, or sense. the
blessing lies easiest on
the silent who talk, the
talkers who rest, and the
reachers-out of hands.

AS THIS RAIN FALLS . . .

for colonel shoup and his lady
their wedding, tuesday, 13 july 1965

the image is so old
one hesitates to use it
        as this rain falls . . .
the image is so old, but
then you begin with the
poem, you end with the poem, and
in the middle, unfortunately,
is not pierre, but the
poem, in which images, as
rain, fall and scatter, run
down the hot streets, bringing
perhaps that one breeze, or
one clap of thunder to bring
us awake, alive, terrified
enough to huddle or speak
out, one clap of thunder in
the single act draining a
man's courage and showing
him his balls—he will
do what is to be done. this
is the fact of marriage, a
summer storm sweeping the
streets, 'til you in any
way whatever respond, yourself,
your own doing, against
the monstrousness we
call life. and in such
response is the measure of
the victory—as this rain falls
i see you taller. as this rain falls
may peace descend.
blessings, friend.

FOR A WEDDING

16 october 1965, for larry and margaret with love

day clear, sun warm,
so new seasons begin,
so the world pulls
together, gathering
itself, while others
march, for good purpose
or bad, for reason
or not.
              men march
driven to it, but
committing one's
person happens
inside.
              clear day
and warm sun brings
the world in, weather
becomes augury.
all men know this,
and some few still
believe.
              some few
still believe a
man must commit himself,
put himself out
before the world, in
warm sun, on a clear
day, when the season
opens before him,
and the world
is around him.

may his face
shine on you
all seasons.

25

FOR A MINISTER

5 june 1966

howard, you
know that the
poem wins, life
wins, in spite of
all.
    nothing the
silly bastards do
defeats anything
important in
the end, any more
than the mountain
wears itself down.
and the air which
carries sand away,
builds someplace
else we move to.

or put it this way:
it is a wedding,
the air and a
mountain. something
will be built, a
new place. people
stand and watch,
and some clap their
hands—for he
maketh the hills to
skip like lambs, and
the mountains to
leap like rams.

26

THE MARRIAGE

28 may 1967, for lewis and anne

it is not god's
business, or ours, what
are we doing here?
they have decided,
taken force in their
hands, will join
themselves. and we all
sit here, staring, smiling,
as if it were our
business, or our
concern. it is not
a societal contract.
it was not made in
heaven. they have
decided. nobody has
put them together but
themselves. and they
will grow by it, looked
at it this way. any
other way is easy, you
garner support. but
this way you make your
own blessings. and
mine follow after, properly,
a distance behind, not
looming on shoulder.
make it. then god and
man will believe
and it will be no more real.

AN ANNIVERSARY

minnie and sam bukberg, 2 july 1967

for the newborn baby the
answer is simple: a large
stuffed gingerbread man. he
will sleep many nights with it.

and for the four year old
goddaughter, the answer is
also simple: a dress. she
is getting class to her now.

and for the newborn's mother,
though a little more
difficult, still, the
friends find a swinging robe,
just the thing to nurse in.

but what shall we do for
this couple, as we wander
through the stores? what can
we possibly buy that would make
sense. my wife is only half
as old as the time they have
lived together. how mount
fifty years simply on a
plaque? they have made their
children, they have their
grandchildren and their great,
and i, who am full of
words, can find none of
the proper ones. the ones
to say, as another did:

> they have fought, they have dug,
> they have bought an old rug . . .

but then, how else to mark it,
that in that time strength
flowed, and warmth. you
do not live fifty years with
another easily, yet it builds,
like the family, a pyramidal
structure, a strong base, the
point piercing heaven. and
the children find it so, home
base, and they walk the stores
fingering table linen, kitchen
ware, books, all the rest,
wondering what home base could
use—could use! after fifty
years!
      nathaniel, kiss your
great grandmother, and show
your smile while great
grandfather holds you in the sun.

FOR PETER AND MARY ON THEIR WEDDING

30 march 1968

one sees a
breast, a head,
in the sunlight, moonlight, it
happens every day if
one is looking.

but to see it, to
live to get
home to it, or
not on the other
hand have to worry.

it's a different
story, something we
come to learn.

relax in it, swim
your life in it, you're
on the maryland shore
and the sun is shining
in your back door
at last.

A WEDDING

8 december 1968, tom and joan clancy

winter is coming. we
bundle up, hurry on our
business in the cold.

the retreats are few,
we all know that, there
are the friends, the pub,
and, if we are very lucky,
a home. the woman makes
that. i am not talking
of domination, or what
they call male chauvinism.
i mean the simple pleasure
of wife and husband. it
is different than lovers'
pleasures, tho they curse
me for corny for it. it

is a pleasure very few
understand, men and women.

the home, the marriage—
it is a sacramental
relationship that not even
the church can deal with.
i have said before it
is nobody else's business,
and i believe god says that
too. it is that contract
made between two people
by themselves, even tho the
state looks on and smiles.
it is that contract we
live by, find energy to
move by, go about our
business,
by, tho
          "the
wintry winds do blow,"

and lets us all find our home.

if the lord lay wisdom on me
this is a blessing. may
it keep you and smile upon
you, may it follow you ever.

FOR JOHN AND RONA

20 september 1969

you hear the news, or
you write it, and
you wish to hell it

was all sports and the
wedding notices, or maybe
the kids being born.
each time something good
happens it gives you
faith, even though it's
as of a grain of mustard.
you keep hoping the
love gets stronger, the
kids better and better,
the world may be saved
after all. you keep
hoping that watching friends
get married, making their
own personal pledge against
a terribly hostile world,
will change things, make
it new, and you hope, and
you give them whatever blessings
you have inside you to give.

A WEDDING

dick and alison burchell, 27 september 1969

water moves slowly, as i see it,
the hudson turgid, despite
a five-knot current. but
it is different in our lives,
we know. the inexorable pull,
the moon swinging the tides around,
the waves rising under winds,
the quick changes. when you
dream of being in water, says jung,

you are in the process of growing,
changing yourself. is it possible,
as i considered in my youth, that
sailors do become wiser than us all,
all us walkers and talkers? is it
possible they come to truths we
can't know? that they find a way
to live—not more easily, none
of us ever really wants that, though
we say it—but more wisely. like
how to settle down, how to find love,
how to give it, simple questions we
all live by. blessings on you, clear
skies, fair wind, and good sailing.

A WEDDING

for gordon and sue, 29 december 1969

like a film it
unfolds, reels
along, and we find
ourselves confronted:
this man, this
woman, facing each
other, hearts full, they
are facing each other,
they are saying the
words, they are committing
themselves to that
particular devotion,
that particular love
they have discovered.
take heart! they are

33

showing us that love exists!
they are showing us there
is some sanity left!
in a world like a film,
they are creating their own
world, they are carving
a space to live in, to
talk to someone else!
may they be blessed for
this, and prosper by it.

A CORNY POEM

for karen and rupert,
on their wedding, 13 june 1970

a day in june.
commitment. confrontation.
it's all we talk about
these days.
and we gather to honor
commitment and confrontation
as old as man and time.
we honor that love that
grows strong enough to
face itself, to commit
itself.
                on a day in june
even the flowers in
my house blooming,
an auspicious beginning
for anything, a start
of summer, facing the
hot sun, facing life.

a corny poem. all we
can talk about, all

we can say: to face it,
to face each other, to
confront, commit, love.
and may the lord bless
you, may the lord keep you,
and may he make his
face to shine upon you.

A WEDDING

for philip and judy, 27 june 1970

they keep walking
two by two, and
we can do nothing
but bless them. despite
all our efforts love
walks right in and
steals the shadows away.
love walks right in
and all the problems
we have dumped in their
laps suddenly become,
possibly, solvable.
they hold hands. they
kiss. the world, suddenly,
is possible. they will
learn differently when they
get older. the youth of
america, casey said, and
spiro said; bums. they are
lovers locked in the
world, and we can do nothing
but bless them, and pray
them happiness, as they
walk into a world less
perfect than they are.

35

FOR JOHN AND LUCY

21 november 1970

aha! spring's a
long way off. the
bears shuffling into
caves. the world
slowing down, the
days gray. one
last fling 'til
sun comes back,
one more time
touching, feeling,
the wedding bells
will ring.
                    the
bears find their
way slowly, they
do not choose quickly,
they spend the
year opting for
this berry, this
particular salmon.
ah, but when the
choice is made!
oh, most true of
all the zoo we are,
the bears.
                    the caves
we sleep in are
the burnished thrones,
our ladies bedazzle
the universe.
                    and
we nose our way

slowly, feeling the
year as few do,
picking the snow or
the spring or the
run of the fish or
the perfection
of the honey straight
out of air. go, let
the dance begin again,
let the cave glow
while the bear and
his lady sing, and
the world turns,
as we do, slowly,
and the spring
begins to build again,
endlessly. it will
greet you to wake
you soon, and
the world will
bless you, with
all its good things.
amen.

FOR NAT AND ELAINE, A BATCH OF SANGRIA

let it foam up, the
good wine, and the
sweet fruit, the
bite of the lime.

life grows happily
that way, cool,
opening, opening.
it supplies the
world, when the

world doesn't supply
it, it sits in its
cool pitcher, waiting
for joy, for peace,
for any kind of
happiness, loud or
quiet, day's
end or day's start,
it is the bubble
of our heart, that
makes us men, reaching
out to another,
learning the universe
is home and not
an alien place.

drink life. grow
drunk on it. spin
and dance. sing.
shout. laugh.
and, even, if it
comes to it, cry.
now it cannot hurt
you, either one of you.
now you can grow
by it. and love.

life carries in it
love, and some of
us do find it.

Birthdays

BIRTHDAYS

my grandmother was born in
'74, my father, '93.
i can grasp both dates.
they're both the same time.
she should be much older.
and your grandmother is
younger than my father.
that's what happens when
you marry a much younger woman.

FOR MY GRANDMOTHER

12 august 1954

the hot sun of
       summer reveals no woman as
              nearly completely as you
reveal yourself, by your
       bearing, your face, your
             actions; nor
seldom has.
       if it please you
            you are my kind
of woman.

you know, as even
       others do, that we
            all bear your stamp, and

i also, who
          am your grandson, youngest
                    son of your
oldest son, i bear that
          stamp as much as any here
                    in this
company. but that stamp, again, is
          on our faces and
                    in the way we
hold ourselves.
          there is another.
                    not one of us
ever soured on life
          enough to say we made
                    a mistake.

you, too, at eighty
          continue as if you
                    were right.
it is good, in a
          bad time, and ensures
                    youth. no one
who married in ever
          understood this, and yet
                    it is as much a
part of our blood as, say, myself
          wearing my mother's
                    eyes, or that
my children
          will be light-haired.

                    you
are eighty, but i have
          to count on my fingers, to
                    figure the year of
your birth, and do not know
          anything other that
                    happened that year.

history does not
            concern me, or rather it
                        bores me, as it should
any live person.
            so, may you
                        remember what it is
you will, either
            pleasant or no, as you
                        decide; i
who am your grandson
            salute you, and offer
                        myself. as in china
you would have my
            life to rule, here
                        i offer it for service, and
for now, this
            verse, words said in my
                        best voice; that
i may learn from
            you not how to
                        live, but
how to move—as you have
            moved, every day, alive in
                        the sun, as the
sun does, today,
            disclose, and in its good light
                        show you.

FOR MY FATHER, ONE YEAR OLDER

7 december 1963

what can i know of it, that
simply, what it is to be born eight
years before mckinley's assassination?
and what has happened in my
life that wasn't earlier disclosed
to him—to be read as he wished,
and pay the piper, too
              he remembers standing at attention
              because his father told him to;
              he remembers god knows what
              of the panic of 1910, the war
              years and the flights as ballast
              in a fabric plane, the boom years
              in the twenties in which he sat
              and filled a royal flush, knowing
              that if he didn't his sons
              wouldn't be born for a while
he remembers everything life
is, and shouldn't be—he knows
by now it is, in general, unfair—and
yet he can look at his sons, the
lives, the various lives they seem
to have made, knowing they all
read books, and—if he has a mind
too—can say: that's enough.
he can say more if he wants to, but
this he knows for sure, his sons read—
there aren't many fathers these days can
say that, and for that we thank him humbly.

FOR A GODDAUGHTER

pretty miss jennifer
sweeter than any
flew through year one
and now it is done,
and two is coming
sweet as honey

          pat-a-cake, pat-a-cake, baker man
          give her a kiss as fast as you can

FOR ANNE

      3 march 1967

        woman, he said, from
        adam's rib,
                woman,
        he said, sarah, serving
        the strangers.
                woman,
        he said, sheba, delighting
        the sage.
            even
        potiphar's wife, he said,
        all created women, all
        that part of life no
        man sees.
            i see, he
        said, and smiled. women
        are the loveliest of
        beasts, said

maimonides, and god smiled
then, too.
                    my girl,
grow with it. today
you are woman.

FOR ANNE

2 april 1967

ah,

burned
in
righteousness
the
heart
doesn't
avail
yet,

another
nucleus
nerves
each.

if
silently

life
inches—
forward—
easily—

any
guy
also
intrudes
no

dice,
even
sevens.
pretty
idiots
turn,
evading

roles.
under
my
old
robe

other
rites

turn,
a
life
emerges . . .

RALPH

22 june 1967

on occasion, he
said, a poem. the
occasion presented
itself. spun

45

on its heel in
the rain, delighted.
a birthday, a
marker in the
best way. a
move. spun on
its heel, ralph
dancing. happy
birthday, he said.

FOR MY FATHER

7 december 1967

we call it a birthday,
that a man has reached
his seventy-fifth, and
we take a drink on it.
we don't ask what it
cost him, the party
is happy. how many
years of how many
hours a day, how
many nights balancing
the books in his
head.
          and the books he
read, and the friends,
and the wearing down, just
by the day-to-day thing,
and the growing stronger
knowing he has lived
justly and loved mercy.

and we are his sons, who
thank him for it.

SUE'S BIRTHDAY

dictated by nathaniel, age 3

what number does her live on
don't type the wrong number 'cause what number does she
       live on
what number
what number
(ssssh)
this one
right
so you won't forget, right

but sue's birthday couldn't be at nigthttime
her going to have a cake
it going to be a big cake
it have to be a big cake

you know what my mom said
my mom said when the cake come i have a sip of her
       iced tea
a little sip
not all of it

when birthdays come then you say happy birthday

PIN THE TAIL ON THE DONKEY

       caravans
       rushing
       up
       in

47

sky—
it's
now

super
unbelievable
splendor
against
non-
"imageable"
sights.

buy
it.
really
take
hold.
do
all
year.

A BIRTHDAY

bertha wasserman, her seventy-fifth

a
unique
nachas,
this—

binding
every
real
thing.

how
aptly
presenting,
plying,
you.

best
in
raising
the
happy
dimensions
about
you,

or
nudging

your
own
unformed
ragtags!

so,
evenly,
very
elatedly,
now,
the
youngsters

find
it
fit
to
hurrah.

APOLOGIA PRO SUA DYLAN

it was my fortieth birthday woke
to my hearing: garbage and neighborhood
and the herring-crested restaurant
where all my poems are read.

still i flow on, like a woman,
and i keep bleeding to prove i'm
alive, and getting angry i haven't
conceived. it was my fortieth birthday.

A TRUNK

for eddie, 30 january 1971

as has been said too
often to bear re-
stating, but not
ever remembered: it
is not the generous
act so much as the
method of giving;
that, so many years
ago i tremble to
remember, he sat me
down in the polo
grounds, handed me
the pearl opera glasses,
and made me watch mel hein;
that i wore so many
suits of his, the whole
damned village thought
i had an italian tailor

name of cozzanetti; that
a trunk with his name
on it serves as my
linen closet now, our
sheets and pillowcases
and towels neatly
folded. the paint is
not bright, it was
painted 1938 i'd
guess to take him
off to college with,
but it sits in my
room, and the name
is there. it's
not the generous act
so much as the method
of giving, a gentle
concern.
            in this
he has never failed
no one, and we thank
him for it—but
i remember most the
hard benches, the man
yelling nest-lee, nest-
lee—the glamour of
learning it wasn't nestle's
i'd been eating—
the pants a little loose
around my waist, a
trunk.
            my linens, my
life, rest in it, thank
you.

FOR FORTY

(a middle-distance race)

don't try more than
twice a night, with
lots of rest and
vitamins.
                eat
well. all
things in moderation.
greet the sun with
a smile, but don't
get bugged about rain.

exercise gently when
up to it. when
down to it, respect
it. love animals
and small children.
don't relate between
ages seven and twenty-four.

be a guru whenever
possible. bars are
good places, also
cocktail parties.

change your hat.
don't change your
underwear or socks.

read little if
at all, but believe
everything. give
answers whether you
know them or not.

grope every girl or woman
in sight, they expect
you to. cackle a lot.

don't sign anything.
stay away from high
insurance rates.
don't learn new tricks.
if you know something
forget it quickly.
write all phone
numbers down.

otherwise it's okay,
but avoid everything.
this too shall pass.

Holidays

HAPPY NEW YEAR

> i thought it would
> be a different place, this
> year at this time,
>
> still the poem promised is
> the poem to be delivered.
>
> sing a different song then
> from the one intended.
>
> ah well if it hadn't been
> the goyim, it would've
> been somebody else, right?
>
> next year, the promised land.

NEW PLACE IN TOWN

> for howard, 17 september 1963

> the way we live these days, there
> aren't enough rituals to
> depend on—or whatever rituals
> there are aren't really helpful:
> it's easy enough to reach
> manhood, but how do you reach for
> a home?

54

what ought to be there
besides some warmth, a few cold
beers in the refrigerator?
easy answers, easy answers, yet
they hold water. my friend we
will never live without knowing
just where it is we are living, just
how the world aligns itself outside
our door.
 so a new house is itself
not as easy an answer as might be
believed, it is a hard answer to
a hard problem, where shall we
live? how construct our lives out
of artifice and simple guile so
as to reach some sort of fullness?

and we pick our houses carefully,
as we grow older, as we pick our
loves more carefully, or even the
simple woman who satisfies our need.
all these decisions raced about,
turned over, turned inside out in
our heads 'til we spin with the
dizziness of it all, we are
ballsy young men, who are not supposed
to be that concerned with where
we live. but we are. and
we find in a broadening horizon more
things to concern ourselves with,
more things to hang ourselves up on;

what we hang ourselves up on
is ourself; constructing our own
debacles carefully also; but to
save us is a care how we live,
what simple things we fill our
life with that we can pleasure in.

and as surely as a man is
lonely, that surely does he
have friends, and that surely
is he capable of founding
a home, making it out of bare
nothings he fights with, filling
a void simply and purely with
care, with an attachment for
whatever his life has to be.

give grace,
then, to a new house,
and peace upon it

A GRACE

bless this house
and all who dwell
safe within its
living hell.

A VALENTINE

direct, in an
iambic or
any other voice,
not one reason
against the fashion

just a particular
openness—
every touch a
live thing

loosely evaluated
over the head of

veritas, verity—
ending sometimes in
silences gone over,

happiest to
effect a
roaring torrent

GRACE FOR THANKSGIVING

22 november 1962

(for a thanksgiving
at paul and ethel's
with love for karen)

the world we may learn to
pass thru, that much
easier, thank you

the day that might open
a little simpler, with
more effort yes, but knowing
what for, thank you

the closer the feeling to
the bone, the closer
bone to brain, the
brain to feeling, thank you

the food eaten better than
before, romantic ain't it
and yet how else to approach
each meal, thank you
        like finding light exists
        like you can enjoy a game

like discovering money buys things
like whiskey tastes good
like love is a pleasure

the simple discoveries none of us
are making, but we might

thank you

A GRACE

for thanksgiving 1963

each year
good food and better friends

each year some new
part of our life to
learn from; each day
we face to grow by;
each day a good
day whatever it
brings:
                strength
against evil; love
instead of anger; friends and
food to face this world
we have to live in,
                lord, for these we pray,
                and for these give thanks

A THANKSGIVING GRACE, 1967

food we sit down to,
giving thanks
                it is
spread before us. we
pray we are worthy, that
survival is not the
only reason we eat. we pray,
like hillel, for one hour
of good works on earth, though
i know i'm repeating myself,
that one hour is too
important to neglect. let us
eat in peace, let the baby
jam his mouth full, while
grandma sees it and smiles,
and the world's power tells
us we are fools, for wanting
love, warmth, food, and peace,
and may we remain such fools.

26 NOVEMBER 1970

for everything we now shall eat
in westbeth and in soho
hand in hand our hearts do beat
like an immortal yoyo

FOR THE NEW YEAR, 1971

wishing i wuz a
cat'lic, so i wooden
hate mendel rivers any

more but say god
bless his soul.
wishing i wuz a
buddhist so i
wooden pay attention,
knowing that his
death will alter
nothing. wishing
i didden have a
hate so big for
what he stood for,
and that he hadden had that
joosh name. wishing
i could drink that
long in life, and
dry out free

OTHER EVENTS

A CHANGE

a subtle altering that
makes no sense at
all, because it
loses us. what
stefansson said about
adventures: things
that shouldn't happen.

Life

F Y I

the day, the
night, man, woman,
the world rolls on
with love, a little
tenderness, it
makes us all
a little better for it,
a little more willing
to meet the day,
the night, each other.

Philosophy

FOR C. B.

19 february 1971

who is clear, who
knows each poem, each
person ought to
have a beginning, a
muddle, and a
end. she could
handle it, she said,
and i believed it.

VICTORIAN HAKKU

i know life is good—
spring will soon be here, tho it's
not yet winter

BALSO'S BLUES

wrap me in your greasy arms, morph,
slide me to sleep
in love's simplicity
it lies, in love's
simplicity we come to a

64

stark determination:
just what it's worth
losing sleep and hard-ons
working our asses off in
vain pursuit, trying
to pursue a trade! love
is a trade, why else settle
for clean shirts or an
evening's good meal. but,
if you won't understand this,
peace on your soul—which
i wanted to uncover, and whose
children i wanted to build slowly
or passionately in
the night and day.

did you imagine that man whose
most unofficial act is the
raising of his manhood would
ever consent to less a definition?
or, able to make paradise
from bread and wine and you,
would find a trade denying it all?

the blues are what song sung.

HELLO THERE

my cough is a little worse
thank you, and we trembled
to hear the report radioed
of the arrest of one hundred
and forty-six vipers. n.
tarnished his pants again
seeking affection. three fights
at the office indicated once more

a refusal to enter the main
event, i.e., whose job am i
after, or, where you
working next week. therefore,
my friend, if you really have
got a boxful, why not bring it up.
nine cops live in this building,
all with trained noses.

DRUNK SONG

there was a breton man
and he spoke the same language
as the clancy boys.
the jews have been
alone so long
no one can talk to them.

EVENTS

we came to it then, and
we went past it. not even
sure we went, passed, came
or did nothing. this is
the secret of it and we
take so long to learn it.
we take so long to learn
anything it makes a man
despair, as if that weren't
passed also. even despair!
we move on but not even

god knows in which direction.
not even god knows.

that is the sum of it,
the man says. and he
knows. in his despair.

if there were another
way no one would take it
in any event, and no one
else would believe it.

TERROR CODDER

burnt umber the color used
in the sicilian mtns, yellow
ochre the color of the
juden star the solomon seal
we worked magics with.
                          the flower the
color of burnt clay, sun-
darkened, or maybe a nipple.

arrange them in a vase.

negromancy said burton the
answer to all ills, are you
a slave of the lamp? baby, it's
dark down there. i was
afraid and did not want to return.

but it is possible to walk across
the ice mountains, or the desert
sands. hot sand to burn your
soles a hard leather brown.

if you make it. otherwise
shrivel. shrive yourself somehow,
it is required by the law.

burnt umber, then, the color
used in the sicilian mountains;
the sardinian women wear
striped skirts, the colors
depending on the particular
locality.
the men
wear tight vests.

THE DANCE AS SEEN

why is it so dark?
why is the light sliding
over walls and faces?
why do her buttocks
move so, and she, her
breasts? why does the
slide show the man up-
side down, and the
lettering backwards.
the music thuds on,
the horn is appropriately
raw. the dancers are
working. hard. and
the dance is seen
in its entirety—a
dance! the men have
taken their shirts off
and the women move faster.
i have seen this dance
before, each time taken,
each time appalled that

68

i am watching, alone.
yet the dances i dance
come on me the same
way, and those i do
dance, shirt off and
moving. it is enough.

THE AMERICAN SCHOOL

what we grind down to isn't dust or a fine edge.
what we grind down to no nub either.
i like the shape of your ass, and
the way your breasts hang.
when a woman has pulled us this far.
when a man has pulled us this far.
they know how to do it, well enough for anyone.

THE SUNDAY COMICS

the spider man attacks
and we tremble in his embrace.
everybody has lousy weather
in the country. postcards
bear strange pictures, the
familiar as well as the exotic.
in his aluminum walker my
son scares cats and kittens,
they scatter before his approach.
we have bred a spiderman between
us, and he trips us up scooting
across the floor. who will save us.

THE MIGRANT WORKERS

and if not god and
goddess, then—then
the old measure holds
true: fit enough at
least to pick blueberries
with you—and therein
lies the answer. the
patch lies before you, ripe
with berries, the two of you
picking like hell—why
not, why not
make a simple god-
damned pie, for once, for
once in your
life. put it on the
table legs sticking
up. a pie. a
simple berry pie.

THE GIFT

with sureness she
irons her
cottons. the colored
and white take
shape. she works forcefully,
tests the heat of the
iron with the tip
of her finger wet
with her spit. skirts with
pleats, blouses both
simple and fancy, dresses.

the finished pile grows.

she knows summer is coming.

PROGRESS REPORT

i'm afraid that facing
reality comes out my
realization this
morning: i have to shave.

i had told her *love* was
in the heart and head and
balls, while *in love* was
a stiff cock and wet
cunt. her girlfriend
agreed with me.
                              difficult,
difficult to fight when
you don't want to hit.
how to teach yourself,
no less the young.

THIS IS STOP TIME

in the marble cemetery
a tree is in bloom already

in the marble cemetery i can see
from my window, pink and white
blossoms of all things assault the
statuary, that's the only way to
look at it. pink and white the tree
stands in the middle of the marble cemetery.

marble itself often pink and white.
is this, then, why the pink and white
tree is blooming, there, in the middle . . .

and breakfast? i'm hungry.

the past that in us all does beat
will be our wine, will be our meat.

TIMESENSE

love an apple
seeds and core
we don't need to
know no more.

lovesong in *a flat*
hot or cold
never will
grow no more old.

vide: all that jazz.

WHAT THE

what the
addict said:
you
got to cold
turkey yourself,
man, nobody else
gone to do it.
or, believe and
you shall be saved,
saith the prophet.
this one, however,
is of neither per-
suasion this time of
year, rather slicing
his turkey cold, laying
the slices haphazard
and piled thick on
the bread into which
lovingly his yellow
blunted hollow teeth tear

yearningly swallowing
harshly and his dry
throat working to swallow
and remembering too late
there is cranberry relish,
with relish viewing
what the

UNTITLED

the man who wrote the
song probably never
knew the truth, but
love *is* a
many-splendored thing

even the wan-ness moves
me but you won't
believe this, and
this sad ass shakes
itself to see you walk.

the belly is part
of it, your sweet
children move me,
a simple prick.

believe it, believe it.
the song sings for
spring as in other
seasons, only more so.

i beat with my
own sap rising, and
watch you from the
corners of my eyes.

73

i turn in bed toward
you and reach across
the void we need to
live in. i reach out
because i love you,
and loving you, can
rarely give, but mostly
take. thank god
you offer. it makes
a perfect match.

the man who writes
the song never knows
the truth. love is
a many-splendored thing.

POSTCARD 37

because we have each been to our
                own hell in our own way and
each hell is disparate
you speak with straight tongue. but
                i am older.
the burn is severer. believe it.
the poems, for example, were unshown
                for a different reason—
you have never been fucked because
                you were famous.
since it's the rest i buy, i will not
                speak of it.

FOUR PHOTOGRAPHS by RICHARD KIRSTEL

A.
the party's over, but
only as billie sang
it, our hearts

breaking as her
voice did, our hearts
lifting like the
dolls are lifted, karen
picks up the dolls, they
are sprawled askew on
the floor, the flanks
of her body shine
before us, her breast
hangs, exposed, the
party's over, but
only as billie
sang it, so long ago,
our hearts breaking.

B.
sexual avarice! desire!
molly bloom saying yes,
i said yes, yes, yes, or
whatever that quote was . . .

karen is about to be
gone down on is the
point. down on! by
a doll! the doll is
going to eat karen! eat her
snatch! endanger that
pussy hidden in her fur!
she is not getting laid.
i am sorry for it! why
is she letting this happen?
why not a man? her tits
are lovely in this picture.

C.
mother, asleep in this picture
with your nipples erected, i
wish we could all rest so

peaceably, i wish our lovers
would sleep next to us
with as little worry.

i wish all ribcages fell with
as clear a definition of life,
and that children could sleep
without suffering.
                              you lie there.
i am looking at you like a voyeur.
i am dreaming of what i will do
when you awake, and then i won't
do it. it's the world we live in,
we can't eat our cake or have it
either. we turn restlessly
all night long, mother.

          D.
          the whore of babylon
          has long legs.

A DIRTY DRAWING

dog fashion's a
bad name for it, derogating
the pleasures of an
ass warm against belly, tits
cupped warm in hand, taking
a different shape as they
do, as snatch does, come at
from that angle, a different
grip, a different pronging and
stroke, and a different
shape, indeed, to the

whole relationship. how
big he is wrapped around her,
how small she curls inside—
the curl the other way an
expanding one, wrapping arms
and legs wide around, the man
big, bulky, making himself
contract inward to her core, here
he *covers* her, she is *taken,* god
knows it may not be as mutual,
but it sure feels good, take and
be taken, cunt throb wet, cock
pulse stiff, breast draw the
hand toward it, ass curl into
belly. only thing missing
is the sweet tongues kissing.

Natural History

THE JOEL L. OPPENHEIMER MEMORIAL GARDEN

is planted in honor
of those who toil
selflessly against
the illnesses that
strike their darling
writers. it is the donor's
hope that they will find
a strength to bear with
crisis here in this
oasis, building and
rebuilding the soul-greatness
that sustains them. no
unwed mothers, please.

the hens and chicks would
like two hours of sun
a day, but even on
none they seem to
manage. this makes them
ideal plants for us.

THINKING

what i am giving you is ex-
actly what i ought to be giv-
ing you but less than
i should be giving you. or
when the armistice sounds
i will want you even more,

when i am not damnably in-
volved in what i ought to be.
that is, it is not always easy
to say what has to be said, or
do the simple acts, sometimes
inside you i wonder (despite my
warnings to you about *that* evil)
why i should deserve it. but
have not stopped fucking you
happily, though why i am
prone to is another story . . .
and loving you i might
understand, possibly, why,
and carefully treading my own
pathways might sometimes say why
are you doing this, taking that
particular step that way, when
you know you ought to be sleeping
hand around her waist, so.

THE SUM TOTAL

the estimates of my
age varied from nine to
almost dead. the little
girl said nine was a
teenager, teenagers
couldn't have children.
the other kid's older
brother said i must be
twenty-two; then
the discussion veered
to religion, mainly
who made babies. my
son soaked it all in,
learning in the gutter.

the catholic beat down
the pragmatist; she insisted
god in heaven made babies,
while he opted for
men and women. in the end, he
weakened, allowing as how
the mother and god made
the baby together, she
down here, he up in heaven.
the questioning began then:
your mother and father
married? my boy insisted
no! then they aren't your
father and mother she
told him. the other
boy's father had a sword and
three guns, he said—how
many your father got?
this was the only time my
son weakened, he turned to
me as i sat on the bench in
the sun, looking the question
at me. none of them saw
my one finger raised to
him in answer. one, he
said. the other boy backed
off. then the little
catholic girl said that
god was in heaven. up
there, the older boy said.
he pointed. that cloud isn't
heaven, my boy said. no,
said the little catholic girl,
that cloud is air—but
do you know who the first
president was? of america?
yes. richard nixon. no,
she screamed, it was
george washington, and

lincoln was . . . as she
paused i prayed she'd
be wrong. the sixteenth!
i'm four and a half,
my son said, in the
march sunlight, 1971.

COME ON BABY

walking out on the street saturday
noon—history which
piles up had not prepared
me, not at all—as in
the worried eyes of the guy
running numbers who had once
worked a proof press with me
a fear grew of where did
he know me from and could
only, stutteringly, ask
did i live here? yes, i answered.

or the fact that the tie
i wanted still lay tangled
in my dark green shirt at
the bottom of the heap on
the chair, and it was that
shirt, too, that i had also
wondered about, not in the clean
shirts, not in the dirty, and
not mine, either, come to
think of it, larry's which
he left here one day when we
thought the world was waiting
for us, and so he took a clean
one of mine. or what is a good

jewish boy doing reading chester
himes and drinking dant on shabbas?

history you who pile up you have
not prepared me for any fact of
my life. who knows what shadows
lurk in the hearts of old girl
friends, for example, that she
should be bugged at my own
admissions finally made of
the hopelessnesses. she could
have laughed it away i suppose
instead of getting hurt—as if
i had slashed her with words, look
out of someone else's eyes her
girl friend said—goddamn it i'm
only human, got two eyes, myopic
and astigmatic, corrected to damn-
near perfect with glasses, whose
eyes should i look out of?

THE KOPF THAT CHEERS

the comforting sound of
the water filling the tub,
the bite of the grapefruit
juice, no, not morning, it's
night, the day's work is
done, the beer and stout
stand on the table and
the glass of them, mixed,
has that guinness face on
it i remember from before the
war—that face and the
dubonnet man—in any
event, night, and the

juice just to clear my
throat, tho it clear my
head too. i remembered the
first time, it was because in
the midst of talking, you
saying no, maybe, no, i,
a little high, said:
when shall i pick you up.
it's enough excuse for a song.

PEOPLE ARE STARVING IN EUROPE

why are they always bringing
me food? italian hors d'oeuvres,
french cookies. what i am
asking is something else, their
own sweet bodies, or in the
one case just keep the hell
out of here. yet the food
piles in. yet if there was
love and you were hungry how
carefully tread asking for a
meal—and buy the food.

but i would still like to know
just what the french cookies
indicated, if not a turn-off
from that particular woman i
wanted to eat, not even like
a gourmet, but, rather, hungrily.
to say, even, i missed it.
but this is not so good to
hear, she would prefer, i
suppose a statement more like
this: i didn't care, i had
other rows to hoe, other

cunts to plow. as she being
woman had her hoes to row,
and plows to cunt.
                              my sickness
is i want to fuck my love and
love my fuck. as i want
to turn my luck into a pack
of tarot, waiting to be
laid out and read. as i want
to find this world a sensible
place. as i want to know
why the french cookies, why
italian hors d'oeuvres, why
rum napoleons, and none of
you brought your cunt along,
or draped it with balls i
didn't wish to be concerned
with. or that vain hope i
keep having that while you
are cooking i'd be buying the
sweet french cookies for the
dessert we would serve while
waiting for the guests to get
the fuck out of there, so we
could concern ourselves with
more relevant matters, rather
than with whether the coffee
is done, and who wants cream
and sugar. you bring yours
and i'll bring mine, and i'll
be in scotland when you are.
then we'll have dinner.

AT ELEVEN-FIFTEEN

          i wonder what that
          tune was, eight years
          ago. we dancing, me

bombed, and the surge
of love so big i
crashed backward
into the wall,
later got violently
sick on the floor.

meanwhile, in 1941,
we danced awkwardly
with louises and
lillians, the wind-up
phonograph, the cactus
needles, bing crosby,
buddy clark, and, then,
sinatra. the girls
giggling as they led
us round the floor.

at night the remotes
came in, nat brandywine
from the roof of
kansas city's best
hotel, or harry kool
from glen island casino.
this poem can never be
finished correctly.

A NOTE FOR THE COMMUNITY BULLETIN BOARD

what people without children do not know
about people with children is that
they are sensitive to the time
children wake up; besides, we
brought our own blankets.

VERITIES

george, in this
life one can't be
right all the
damned time. i
hate those corn
muffins i bought
for breakfast. they
did not taste good
to me. they did
not taste good to
me. damn it, they
did not taste good
to me at all.

ODE TO A STUDY AT LAST

alex has invented a
nite table, and my old
lady cleaning, and i have
a desk in a room with
windows and a plug for
light.

THE ONLY ANARCHIST GENERAL

the architecture fell into
place only at night, the paths
led somewhere, the lights
lit them, even the low
wall had a reason finally,
it comforted me walking.

my wife questioned my
orders as if i wasn't a
general. the bridge still
frightens me, *not* the ravine,
which is why it is necessary
to make friends with trolls,
constantly. still, i met my people
halfway home, and walked back in company.

my wife questions my orders as if i
were not the only self-taught happy
genius of my household. i note
crests and rises, point out
defensible positions. the
armies move and swell, the
battle is coming. my wife
questions my orders. i am an
anarchist general shouting orders in a
strictly formed landscape. my children
did leave me here knocking on wood,
i walk the bridge alone in the night's
landscape, thinking of low
walls, covering the terrain.

BOOK REVIEW

i woke in the middle of
the night, heard the voices
talking? laughing? fighting?
enraged, i went back to
sleep. seven out of nine,
she said, stories end in
drunkenness or sleep. there
is no resolution.
                    and they
won't understand it, won't
understand it at all!

the man who sleeps and
cannot sleep, the man who
dreads sleep, who dreads
awakening, who can't go on
from tiredness and yet cannot
get to sleep, who drinks to
sleep, and cannot sleep for
drinking, who envies soft
susurrus of the sleep of
others, who twists i have
said over and over in his
bed all night, they do not
understand the resolution
asked, in simple sleep.

THE LADY ACROSS

the lady across the courtyard
has only objected twice: while
the convention in chicago was
going on she yelled about loudness;
then when we talked about ladies
taking their blouses off, letting
their tits hang free, she screamed
again. yet we've had the late show
on much louder, and we've fucked
noisily by the same open window
time after glorious time.

THE LADIES OF WESTBETH

I.
because you were seventeen when
we met, i was older then. fourteen
years difference is fourteen years
difference, but seventeen is a

special age for women, and your
pale flesh sent me leching across
long island, holding your hand on
beaches, straining my eyes when the
bikini shifted. you were young then,
i've always been one who lusted for
pretty young goyim, the thin
blondes turning tan in the summer sun.

then you turned twenty-eight and
i went past forty. i talk to you
now by the elevator, discussing our
various interests; i even tried touting
you onto our cat, to take her along
with your two, getting her out of my
marriage bed. because i'm happier
with my lady, no doubt of it, and
the leching is gone—but still it would
have been nice, baby, if you'd seen
more than the dirty old man, if you'd
taken your bathing suit off, balled
me, even answered my call, or thanked
me for sending the poems.
                              instead you
brought me your own poem ten years
later, no longer a pretty blonde goy
teasing the horny poet with sweetness,
sweetness of seventeen-year-old flesh
tanning away in the summer sun. why
should i care about your mind, lady?

II.
your daughter now lounges around
this building turning all of us on.
one day she said that i knew you,
she said that i used to run with
her mother. so i found out
that you had a kid when i sat
as a junior member of the board.

frankly, i didn't want to come on, then,
but the thought would occur, late
at night. everybody else in the
bar was making out, why shouldn't
i? that's how it was in the good
old days. now i don't want any
either, but like to tease your
daughter because young women
are pleasures in any event.

III.
you were eleven, your sister nine or
ten; i was an early twenty. old
as i thought i was i was still
a kid. the difference was that
you knew your own age. now your
son plays with mine, your husband
and i talk about the meaning of
habnab and somewhere twenty years
have gone up the flue, under the
bridge, disappeared. if you watch
the kids this afternoon, i'll
take them tomorrow morning.

IV.
your ex-husband maligns me in
his books, turns my first
wife into what he wanted you to
be; you walk in the yard with
strange men and big dogs. your
son can talk to me, your daughter
has the biggest tits in the building.
i used to think about yours, while
my first marriage was breaking apart.

V.
you were standing on
the corner and i
passed by at first

not recognizing you.
after all it was
ten years ago. like
we say we aint gettin
any younger. in the
morning, with the
coffee cooking i put
my arms around you.
why are you romantic
in the morning you
said. i couldn't
quite believe it.

which makes me think
it was just as well
altho that is a
bitterness we're not
allowed to have. i
would have felt much
better if i had known
that quiet line right off
passing by the corner.
why *am* i romantic
in the morning?

THE BODY POLITIC

halfway between
night and morning.
middle night.
soft haunch of
thigh. cushion,
as noted before,
derived from
the word for
thigh. persian?
i don't know, know

only the ease of
soft haunch of
thigh, middle
night. halfway
between young and
old, mid-age. too
old to do, too
young not to
want to do. the
poisons erupting
through the flesh,
the body politic
revolting, casting
its poisons, boils,
carbuncles, all
manner of fevers.

halfway between
pity and rage all
at one's self, cursed
for what's not
done, cursed for
what is to do.

the white meat of
tender haunch mixes
with gigot roti,
properly pink and
tender, next to
white beans, and
one avoids other
images of meat. this
is enough to stop
sex and eating, crossing
each other. leave
the rest of the
acts for yourself.
they are little enough.

if i could i would
drink this all out.
that doesn't work
just now, not even
watching the wine
being poured, just
as the blue lines
carry the blood
beneath the
flesh of the
thigh. i promised
not to speak of
blood spurting,
but what of the
juices of the
gigot, in the
plate, next to the
white beans? what
of the middle
night? what of the
pull in two directions?

which way with the
body politic turning
each way, rotting
a little each
time the decision
is made, what about
the body politic i
promised also not
to speak of, the sins
responsible for
committed or not?

i am too old, or
i am too young, and
the body does not
know what to do,

which choice to make.
the body's confused.

god help us, maybe
the first choice
was right, it is
the soft thighs
will save us, if
we can get past the
other images of flesh,
if we can forget
what we do to
blood, if we, for
god's sake, stop
doing it, and
once again turn
human, in middle
night, in mid-age,
in all the turnings
of the body and
the head, in all
our twisted reasoning.

THE NEWS

she'd been sick three
weeks, couldn't cook, couldn't
stand the raw food, her
stomach settling down only when
finally supper got a little
food in her
                    when the doctor
called, the diagnosis confirmed,
motherhood again, she
ate all my strawberry cheese
napoleon, then told me.

MY OLDEST SON

          it's not only that you're
          handsome in the color
          photo your class picture—
          it's that already you
          have look of man, a
          western man, cowboy, that
          about the lips there shows
          a resoluteness, a solidness of
          purpose. it well could
          make one worry. then, too, you're
          handsome as your mother, so
          what is one to make of that?
          and you're close to ten,
          closing in on my own
          age. i rode my old
          bus not two months ago,
          back home, passed joe nocco's
          house where he, kenton, george
          chase, myself, at fourteen
          decided to get drunk. i
          remembered that night, and
          remembered you at ten are
          just four years away from
          where i was that few short years
          ago. i hope it's easier for
          you, though i know it
          can't be. we have done
          nothing for you besides
          father you and occasionally
          support you.

                    but there was
          one day i showed you how to
          walk through the tail of
          a hurricane, and i know there
          was a christmas when you

got your trains, and in that
saddest, simplest fashion of
fathers, i feel better.

                    maybe,
in the end, the job was done,
maybe even better than my poor
father who never showed a
son of his what man was; and
though i delude myself and
know it, i would like to think
that thin-lipped mouth looking
out at me comes from me, even
with none of my own to offer save
in my own view of me. maybe things
do grow, develop, maybe, even,
one makes better than himself,
sometimes, in the end, in
color photos of his son.

LIBERTY

A SONNET

i cock my legs up in the midst of it.
the nuts. that's what it is,
the nuts. the way cranach
drew eve's belly,
pregnant in the garden of eden.
when the baby kicks
it's the nuts. the nuts.
so live with it, he said, as sweetly
as the big boy's piss is
when he displays it. in the midst
of his red leather hassle.

Art

SUNDAY AT HIGH NOON

it will be erected.
thirty feet high in the
sun. a thirty-foot
erection, with no
chance for love, going
into a long depression,
or a deep one. how
could he do it? besides,
it ain't an erection
at all, it's a lot of
damned triangles, all
tied together, and, as
ovid could tell you, a
triangle is worse even
than a useless erection.

INTERVIEW

it's where we live.
he asked, in all his
glory as reporter,
is it possible i could
see roi jones, the writer?
he's just another fuckin
nigger to us, the man said.
finally, i thought, leroi'd
be delighted, but the others
wouldn't. i'm not. that's
a fuckin cop. he don't

like nothing. he says what
he likes and i can't, not
to him. he's got the gun.
and governor hughes thinks
this man is protecting
us. he really believes
that. he really believes
that. leroi may not be
protecting america either
but governor hughes don't
believe in him. governor
hughes believes the red
cross is protecting america
too, but they are giving
the emergency supplies to
the whites. this also is
a final solution: let
them starve. they brought
it on themselves, didn't
they? like the old friend
who today finally reached
the line. you know, he
said, leroi is capable of
that kind of thing, guns
and violence. yes, i
said. leroi *is* capable of it.
but i knew it when i
met him. it was not a
condition of friendship.
nor is it how to measure
friends. but i know i too
might reach a line with leroi.
i hope it is a reasonable
one. like if he blew up
my house or stole my child.
i do not think i will
abhor him because governor
hughes thinks he is immoral.
i think that where we live

is a dangerous place because
in the end the citizens think
uniforms will defend them,
and that guns firing one way
are better than guns firing
the other, and that there
is justification for
lumping all men together.

HOMAGE TO NICANOR PARRA

anyone who invites seventy
poets to meet gets exactly
what he deserves; any poet
who accepts is equally
foolish.
        yet, you, my friend,
were the undeserved bonus—
your poems and your self.
gracious in meeting me, still
your eyes wandered across my
wife appreciatively, a true
connoisseur. when yevtushenko
did that i got mad because i
do not trust his view of the
world or the way he looked at
her, but our view of the world
coincides: it is woman, no
matter what else we talk about.

i must also say it is a long
time since i have found something
new in a poem—my friends
gasped, saying, joel, if anything
he's closer to the new york school!
my friends, it is closer to the
poem. it's not a mistake in

direction, either, my friends,
it's that he's right too and i
didn't know it 'til now.

a provincial new yorker, what
did i know of chile save the
dreams during childhood romances,
and, later, vague references drifting
in through conrad. i knew the
galapagos tortoises lived hundreds
of years and they belonged to chile.
what image to make of that! and,
every time i look at the map of
antarctica i see that chile claims
a slice.

        you and i, we have spent
our lives, in new york and chile,
loving women, hating women, having
our hearts broken and repaired by
the cherub at the corner. now, you're
fifty-five and when i mention my
nineteen-month old son, your eyes
glint, and you know you have me—
i have, you say, one seven months
old. all that's left is to bless you.

HOW TO APPROACH BLACK ART

(a statement prepared for and read at
a P.E.N. panel discussion on:
HOW TO APPROACH BLACK ART in
spring 1971)

wheah! it's when the
drums stop . . .
or, does it need to
be approached?

men write, that is the fact.
black men write, also
a fact. the kids
write, when the men
allow it.
                    parochialism a
virtue when necessary,
allowing growth, then
you move on to other
parishes. other pariahs.
how else do you learn
except by straw men and
windmills, and your own
coterie, at least for
that first start after
the inward one. item:
starts inside oneself, the
only one writing. moves
to the group, your friends.
understood, your enemies.
moves out, the world.
art is one thing,
black is another,
black art is or isn't.

to read something because
black man wrote it? sometimes,
but for art? sometimes.
not often. to read it
because it is written,
yes. is it art then?
sometimes. pick up
a book and begin. sometimes
ask what color the writer,
sometimes not, but that's
all sociology, yes? maybe.

art is a bad word, but
do rain dances or sand

paintings qualify? when they
good enough transcend, whatever
that may mean. read! read!
read! or don't. sometimes
better. kids write sometimes
and i can only tell them about
what sometimes. if they
have to know they are black
they will write black. is bad?

POEM FOR THE STATE

from "OF ASPHODEL,
THAT GREENY FLOWER"
by William Carlos Williams

My heart rouses
            thinking to bring you news
                        of something
that concerns you
            and concerns many men. Look at
                        what passes for the new.
You will not find it there but in
            despised poems.
                        It is difficult
to get the news from poems
            yet men die miserably every day
                        for lack
of what is found there.
            Hear me out
                        for I too am concerned
and every man
            who wants to die at peace in his bed
                        besides.

which the old man said, dying
himself. which we all know
sooner or later or die for
lack of it; only in dreams
he puts before us does
man live.
                make no mistake
about it, there will be
poems and songs and dances,
paintings, all of it, like
it or not, no matter what
the culture says or does.
but the culture carries no
such guarantee, it comes,
it goes. it might do
well to wonder which is
needed for the other's
life. men make both
states and art. one lasts.
the other lasts only as long
as it allows for art—
a simple view, but it
has held up a long, long
time. only the statue
of ozymandias stayed on,
the poet told us, only
the glory that was
greece, the grandeur that
was rome. by bits and
pieces we put the world
together, always.

STAMPED PAID

no glances at
kings, rather
garbled
images,
also
     discrete
          paths
              paths
                 toward
                    a
                      man's work

oh the bird halfchewn by
the friendly dog, it
lay outside on the
doormat, by which i mean
to imply no values or
judgment thereof, any more
than if i cited
dream-images of doctors
with rosebud vaginas in
place of reflectors.

also, it is true, no
matter what age, to have
been only the dregs, or
the refuse, or the
disenchanted, or the
forlorn, or the ones
who copped out . . . dogs
will chase birds.

POEM FOR WESTBETH

26 may 1970

stone
upon stone we
build buildings.
or clay. or
wood, adzed or planed, or
bricks. they are
piled up. the
world grows, each
seeking a house, a
space, a place to
do, build, make, think,
or more simply, live.

the world turns on
this even if there
are too many of us.
what shall we do?

the man said to me
why not for the really
poor, and the woman,
why should you have it
and we not, just because
my husband's an engineer?
the answer to the
woman was easiest. helen
married a poet, and aside
from the family, this was
the only good thing
that happened. the answer
to the man took a
long time.

107

                    i believe in
the necessity of poets,
and even when dancers
wake me up at ten sunday
morning i believe in them.
and when the car hauler
full of junked heaps pulled
up along bank street i
thought oh my god a sculptor's
moved next door, but i believe
in them too. the culture
depends on its artists—
whether we are out hunting
for food, or trying to stop
a war. and i sit in
my room guilty, wishing
everyone could live there,
and yet i say damn it,
i can, i'm entitled,
as long as i do my work.
and i pray god that only
painters move next door
because poetry is a silent art,
and then i pray god that
they all continue, gloriously.

POEM FOR SOHO

8 june 1970

i am his majesty's poet at westbeth;
pray sir, whose little painter are you?

and i notice in the news that
the kids are still being encouraged

to take part in the system, and
that the seven green berets dead
today of a misplaced dynamite charge at
fort bragg or wherever it was are
more heroic than the new left bombers
and i wonder why we persist in pursuing
that vain dream: a space to work in.

but, damn it, we do persist, the
work keeps coming out, and all we
are asking is a little cave somewhere,
where we can do the work. even
cro-magnon allowed that, and,
possibly, even gained by it.
at least we think they found where
the animals were, by the paintings.

if only we could find our consciences
as easily. this is the fight we
are fighting. and asking for
space to build our own perimeters
in defense of such. believe us,
or drop the history of man.

POEM FOR WESTBETH

16 december 1970

in this season, quietly, one
asks for peace, and
good will. we do not
always receive. sometimes
it's that bundle of
sticks they kept

threatening with. we
ask, over and over,
each new year.
                    it
comforts me at such
times to see hanging
on my wall what mr.
conrad told us once:

> ... the only saving grace that is
>   needed
> is steady fidelity to what is nearest
> to hand and heart in the short
>   moment of each human effort . . . .

and i bend again to
the wish, and the will
to implement it, and
smile on the children,
who believe.
              they believe
it can happen. seeing them,
i pray that it will. peace
on earth, and to men,
good will.

FRAGMENT FROM THE WORKS OF ANACREON

recently discovered in a cairn by the river
meander and translated particularly for a
festival of poets at the state university of
new york at stony brook

quote to me from homer if you must;
read me the rules how a poem is made;
but don't, i beg you, tell me back sober
what i spent a good drunk convincing you.

110

listen to my meander, but not with your
(stylus (?)); listen with your ear,
and fight with me if i am wrong.

the stonecutter will not put up with
a care-less apprentice, and i do not
want to talk to a teacher with no ideas.

. . . . and i curse and
drink harder. you cannot explain this.
neither does homer care what rules
of action you have contrived for him;
he also got drunk when the need was there,
and sang good songs for the rest.

Politics

AMERIKA, THE BEAUTIFUL

Oh, beautiful for specious lies
for somber yields of grain
for poison-tainted travesty.
above the blighted plain.
Amerika, Amerika, god's turned his face from thee
and crowned thy greed with stunted seed
from tree to dying tree.

THE MORNING AFTER

wednesday, 8 november 1966

okay all you crass cocksuckers in
queens, and all you alabama cow
fuckers, and you christ-struck
faggots in california, you
got your dream, and now
we can forget our god-head.

andy jackson and tom jefferson better
forgive you, nobody else can. you've
sold your freedom to the first
man come along to be your savior,
you don't even see the country
oozing out from under. well,
like ronald reagan said about the
california state lands if you've seen
one tree you've seen em all—

                                    look,
it's not only that the niggers don't
count, it's that the bill of rights
don't count, democracy don't count,
morality don't count, decency, care,
concern, thought, life, and sundry
other minor affairs don't either.

it's that this city now can be
a police state—that's where
the rub is, like hitler, you just
pass a law to make it legal. easy as
pie, and who cares where the country
went, the whole damned idea, the whole
thing we think we're fighting for
over there.
                    "man is born free and
everywhere he puts himself in chains."
everywhere he asks for it, says take me,
stick it in my ass, break my balls,
and opens his mouth when they piss on him.

let us pray.

SOME CHILDREN, KANSAS, ONE NIGHT, OTHER THINGS, ANOMALIES

on the night when what was left of the
good things came to an end, i called
new mexico. i am always calling somewhere,
but birthdays are different. the older
one answered, and i found at thirty-eight
i had a son with a bass voice. kansas
was voting and so was nebraska.
                                    i can't
even get angry anymore, i'm tired,

they have taken the country away. who
cares? who can care anymore? even
karl shapiro is writing "frankly
erotic" poetry!
                    now american flags will
fly everywhere. what happened? they
never saw a black man, and they believe
that the air they breathe is pure.

meanwhile, the simple fact is that strom
delivered and mayor daley didn't. i
hope it is remembered. what could i
tell that boy with the bass voice, or
his brother who had just turned thirteen,
or, even, the new one here, two, running
nose, not only not knowing why i had
brushed him off my lap to follow the
night, but not even knowing yet how to
blow his own goddamned nose, offering
it up to me, dripping, over and over to be wiped.

what shall we do? what shall we do? shave?
settle down? shut up? pack the bags?
will there still be passports? o my people,
my poor dear father convinced that i'm
wrong, anthony imperiale convinced he is
right, spiro t. agnew convinced he's vice-
president and deserves to be . . .
                              and
why not marry the richest man in the world?
why not? why not be a sixty-two year old in
queens celebrating by firing your rifle with
the arms cache inside the house—and why
not give up the dream, move out, take
your children with you, go? why not?

in "one of the most closely fought
elections in american history" who
really gave a damn, save the worst?

114

gentleman, i give you the president
of these united kansas.

NAPALM POEM

tomorrow is groundhog day.
when i poke my head out of the burrow
what will i see?

sons off to the west,
and one i neglect here at home.

women i have balled
not to their own satisfaction.

women, countless, i have turned
onto numerous perversions.

students i have not taught.

bosses i have given no work, and

friends i take money from.

i do not think any of these
have burned scars ribbing their bodies.
i do not think any of these
says oppenheimer go home.
i do not think they writhe
cursing my sins.

perhaps i am wrong
let them come forth.
let them arraign me. let them
curse me with bad dreams.
let the heavens open up and rain

down on me, my sins, those i have hurt.
let my sleep be bad. let my
appetites disappear. not one of them
has died or lived crippled because of me,
even tho i be a dirty-minded poet. they
have grown, somehow. they live, somehow.

i know you will not listen, you
have made up your minds. it
burns me up the way they carry on, you say.
i know this. i ask you to think just once
of what you are doing. fuck up a woman for love,
that is a better crime. fuck up a
child for love. that is a better crime.

napalm, napalm, burning bright
in the jungles and the night
what immoral hand or eye
framed that searing body's cry?

MORATORIUM

wednesday, 15 october 1969

the little boy wasn't three yet,
and as the crowd grew, carrying
candles, it was hard to know what
he thought about it. he, himself,
wasn't carrying a candle but had
a large corrugated cardboard whale,
it had giant teeth, and he held it
high and proud. four people looked
at it and said noah the whale, and
one oohed moby dick, but most didn't

116

say a thing. it was a silent march.
the little boy got tired, but he would
keep walking, so he gave the whale to
his father. now it rode high above
the crowd; people were asking what
is it? and, why carry a whale in
a peace march?
                              i tried to answer
that they were dying more quickly than
us, so it seemed to make sense. some
looked at the two of us very strangely,
a few heard what we were saying.
                                            they

are killing the whales so fast that
the fleets come back half-full ahead
of time—and a male blue whale can
swim his whole life without ever
finding a mate. this should tell us
what sort of a beast we are, how we've
learned to draw leviathan forth from
the sea, and kill him. from the
beginning we knew how to kill ourselves.

SOME QUESTIONS FOR TODAY

15 november 1969

were the rocks thrown first or
the tear gas? does it matter?
if spiro was right why did all
the media keep talking about the
couple thousand in dupont circle
with only one mention of the six
thousand praying in washington

117

.

cathedral? if it was raining and
cold, why did three thousand people
still find themselves capable of
lying down in the mud at central
park?
            why was tricky dick muttering
while the rocket went up? why did
the rocket go up? why does the
spokesman for the catholic war vets
think that all the people out today
are "professional demonstrators"?

not even jefferson or walt whitman
can answer these questions no matter
how strongly they believed in us,
and although we all hope for our
salvation through our belief, no one
on this black earth can forgive any
of us for what we have done to it,
what we have done to ourselves. let
each pray for himself, for peace,
let each pray for this world.

ANTI-SEMITISM

for albert shanker, the adl, et al.

hey jewboy with or without yommikah
this is a jewboy speaking

jeremiah, isaiah, the first joel,
they could say this came from
g-d, i can't use that cop-out, i
can only call it truth.

118

                        i am indicting
you all for a grievous sin, that
of having learned nothing. the
blacks, o my people, are not
cossacks, they are not burning
the shtetls, they are not building
buchenwalds, they are not englishmen
lighting the pyres, or spaniards
with thumbscrews.
                        you are fighting
the wrong fight. i say you though
one of us because i will not—
remembering that all except judah
and his brothers thought the greeks
were right. judah won.
                        why
are you not crying out, instead
of pissing and moaning? why
aren't you fighting the good fight?
why are you not admitting that
a fifteen year old girl in harlem
might have good reason to believe
us evil, when you have kept your
mouths shut all the while your
white friends kept saying we were?
she bought whitey's lesson just
as shamefully as you, is all.

                        this poem is also directed to
                        micks whose fathers fought at
                        the post office; poles,
                        ukrainians,
                        and lithuanians who fought the
                        russkis; russians who fought the
                        czars; greeks who fought the
                            turks;
                        eyetalians who remember
                            garibaldi;
                        and any man who believes in

                              honesty and decency, freedom
                                    and
                              the right to life.
                                            thank you.

POEM WRITTEN IN AND FOR NEW YORK CITY

            the blue whale and the
            sperm whale are dying.
            only the children
            can tell us this.

            the wolf is an
            "endangered species,"
            spending his life with
            the stronger bowing
            to the weaker in any
            internecine battle.
            only the children can
            tell us this.

            the air is dying, every
            breath catching harder.
            only the children can
            tell us this.
                        the water
            at the beaches may or
            may not be fit to swim
            in this summer, they say.
            only the children can
            tell us this.
                        the noise
            pounds on the head, which
            leads to madness. this is
            provable, but only the
            children can tell us this.

120

people are dying from hunger.
only the children can tell
us this.
people are dying from
napalm. only the children
can tell us this.
people are
dying from bullets and bombs.
only the children can tell
us this.
children are dying,
killed by other children, or
by men hired for the public
safety, and again and again
and again only the children
can tell us this.

thank god
they do. thank god they
have learned how stupid we are,
all of us, out after our piece
of ass, or money, or fame.

i cannot say that i am
proud of my life as i
drink another bourbon,
but i am proud of the
children, and i grieve
that they die while we
live, and that we have
to depend on the
children to tell us.

no child ever dug an oil well,
but many have tried to
get through the core of
the earth to get to china.
as any child will tell you.

HARVEST MOON

by accident, i guess, it
all pulls together. today
i asked, when is the harvest
moon? you're in it, baby,
she said. you are in it.

so the recipe came out:
take one towheaded kid.
name him leif. then that
polish baron, or whatever
his name rank and serial number
was—kosciusko?, no—
pulaski, that's the guy.
add a genoese jew named
improbably columbus. mix
them all together they
spell melting grass, while
the pablum keeps stirring
on the stove.
                    oh my
beloved country! thank
your beloved prez!
he's filled up october!
he's satisfied all the
minorities! the ninth of
october! leif ericson!
the eleventh of october!
pulaski! the twelfth of
october! cristoforo
colombo!

            if we could only
sneak in augie belmont
on the tenth, while crispus
attucks creeps through
the weeds, firelock at the

ready, and chaim, dear
chaim, keeps emptying his
purse.

             sing ho, spiro, sing
ho for the melting grass—
but watch out for greeks,
and beware the militant
quakers. it was all
in another country, and,
besides, the wenches
are dead. and here comes
another religious caterpillar.
and there goes another
bloody dream, stirred into
pablum. the dream, the
dream, that is too dirty
to have. that all those
nasty nasties, all those
corrupters of youth,
say it's all right
to dream. up your
permissiveness he
says my friends and
the multitudes cheer.
and won't let their
son eat when he's
hungry, they promise,
and won't give him
strawberries and cream
even when the revolution
comes.

             well, i know
what's good for me, and
wish to shine, perishing
republic, or even
harvest moon, on, on,
up, up. lighting

the match under the
spoon my pablum
cooks in, the belt
tightening round my
neck, the veins
standing out.

                you got
maybe a cookie, the
hemlock's so good?

the senate voted today
that pornography is bad.

sixty senators are
worried about its
long-range effects.
long-range? at six
inches? which is
far enough range for
any bomb. ah . . .

shine, perishing
republic, the boats
are launching in
greenland, spain, even
the heart of poland.
eat. grow strong.
discover the country
you live in. shine
on harvest moon.

AS WE GO MARCHING ON

the last time was
1932. they were
asking for bread.

mr. macarthur wore an
english-tailored
uniform with hand-
embroidered insignia,
and set the american
record for rows of
ribbons with seven.
he sat on a horse.
the veterans in the
bonus army, they
threw stones and he
did not once flinch.
this was reported in
his obituary in the
times. there were
also some machine guns
and some tanks around
him. douglas macarthur
was an american hero.
no one ever had to
tell him his duty.

one hundred members
of the eighty-second
airborne said they
would throw down their
arms and join the
demonstration if ordered
to fire.

           how many rows
their medals make? how
many purple hearts to
weigh down your blouse,
general? out front,
how many hands never no
more to stitch in
silver and gold the
insignia of a general in

125

the united states army?
how many legs not to
wear high polished
boots? how many men
growing saigon bluegrass
to feed your horse to
put your rump on? what
do you die for, general?

THE PURSUIT
of HAPPINESS

THE WAY IT IS

how much
you
        talk,
how much you
fuck it
            up. why
baby you
got the world at

your finger tits.

Fun

SOME SUGGESTED GUIDELINES

from DADDY
(Drunken Admiring Daddies on Delinquent Youth)

this is a bar.
see the bar. see the drunks.
some are hungover.
that is reprehensible.
nevertheless it is why they are here.
at home you may run and jump and scream because it is
    your house too.
even if it is your daddy sitting at the bar you should behave
    decorously.
if you don't daddy should get you the fuck out.
especially if there are many hangovers around.
or a football game.
or anything.

also you should not bug the bartender.
he is your daddy's friend and is worth not bugging.
otherwise he may cut your daddy off.
if, on the other hand, he likes you, he will let your know.
he might even give you a ginger ale with a maraschino
    cherry.
maraschino cherries are the red things in the old-fashioned
    glass.
an old-fashioned glass is a special glass for old-fashioneds.
old-fashioneds are a special kind of drink.
maraschino cherries are red because of the poison they
    treat them with.

129

shut the fuck up and get away from me.
bug your mother for a while for christ's sake.

also don't throw the nice ball when no one is expecting it.
people have heart attacks.

also don't fight with another kid when in a bar.
only adults are allowed to do that.
it is a SLA regulation.
besides the bartender does not know how to handle it.

also don't play with the ice when customers are around.
some adults have very queasy stomachs.

in fact, if you do come in, just say:

> hello papa.
> hello uncle (insert
>   name).

then, if applicable, add:

> do you have a present
> for me?

then, say:

> good-bye papa.

and leave.

LA HUELGA

for j. bouton and the players association

this is a revolutionary poem for
ballplayers. willie mays hit me a
homerun. hank aaron hit me a home-
run. cleon for god's sake please

130

hit me a homerun. ziegel if you
score it wrong you're dead.

and it has never occurred to the
owners that we went to see the
players play, and nobody ever cared
whether or not connie mack was
sitting in the dugout. we didn't
even care about miller huggins! how
do you like that—the fans didn't
care about miller huggins!

the fans cared about something else.
like maybe the well-hit ball. like
maybe the well-thrown ball. like maybe
the ball well-played. the owners
never understood that.
                          so don't play.
don't go out on the field. sign
football contracts. or i'll buy you
a drink. that won't help either; but
nothing ever helped in my own bad jobs,
with the bosses raking it in, except
that knowledge inside that you were
the only one knew what you were doing.

THE ALL-STAR

the weight of the petals
makes them fall
one two three four
the first was
outside, the next two, low

the last crossed the plate
a little inside

"that would have been nice
   that would have been something at a time
      like this
   i wish i had, to tell you the truth
   but maybe it's better i didn't swing
   i might have been embarrassed
   i might have popped it up."

AND ON THE SEVENTEENTH DAY

the truck driver said of
course they win, they got
seven years' practice!
                    and the
magic was working all over the
bar: i changed seats every score
and it worked! cleon held the
last catch like he couldn't
believe it, and nancy seaver
is pretty, but why couldn't
we see anybody else?
                    and why
was a ball bouncing off
robinson's glove a hit, while
all our guys got errors?

and cleon said, deadpan, in
the clubhouse, after: don't
you know, man, don't you know
good pitching always beats
good hitting?

ZEN YOU

as we were involved in this
dart game where nobody seemed
able to hit the bull's eye, which
was necessary to end it, i
turned to my partner and said if
i use zen, that is to say, if i
worry only about the dart and
allow the dart the problem of
the target, perhaps?

                        good
christ no! he shouted—worry about
the fucking bull's-eye and let the
dart take care of itself, for
christ's sake.

                i took aim, carefully.
the dart flew straight to the bull's-eye.
oh well, this is the west, we
do things differently, i suppose.

Games

RED STAR OVER CHINA
(to the air "yankee doodle")

the winter geese are flying.
the stone mason's wife
sits alone by her window.
he is far to the north
under the red star of china.
she eats her mo shui.

THE ILIAD

in a somewhat condensed transliteration for
modern readers

helen had a snatch
all filled with honey;
paris had a ball
was made of money.
they went off to
ball and joy—
that was the start
of the fall of troy.
(she was stolen away
from the king of greece—
it caused more fussing
than the golden fleece.)
agamemnon called
his boys all in,

said, yessir boys,
got to stop their sin.
all the gang
from near and far,
including lads
without one scar,
jumped in the boats
and started to paddle;
hector started oiling
his boots and saddle.
most got hurt,
a lot were dead,
but helen ended
back in aggy's bed.

this proves a moral
often told:
ain't nothing finer
than a custom rolled,
but of all the
most unkindly cut
is got for smoking
another's butt.

BIG AYE POEM

she moved; my spirited soul arose,
zoomed about a while and lit its nose,
turned into a drugstore and stayed a bit,
somersaulted down her neck, past her left tit;
considered the situation already canned,
and, the fire of love lit, sat and fanned.

17 MARCH 1963 IN THE PARK

the menstrual girl from the bronx has come,
in the ranks of the beat you will find her;
her father's word which she guided on,
she has long since left behind her.

AH, THESE UNGENEROUS LOVERS

it is in her bed
her ass is at its best,
likewise her rosy box,
and her maidenly breast.

it is in her bed she finds
a peace that passes under handling,
and, turning to the other side, wishes,
i suppose, for just a girlish candling.

THE ACT

as i do
it is as it is
does as it does
as i am it is
is as is is as
i do as i do
as it does as it
does as it is
as is is